MORE GHOSTS OF ERIE COUNTY

by

Stephanie Wincik

Copyright 2005 by Stephanie Wincik

ISBN 0-9725650-2-7

All rights reserved. No part of this book may be used or reproduced in any form without the express written consent of the author and publisher, except in the case of brief quotations embodied in literary articles and reviews.

This book was printed in the United States of America.

Published by One Horse Press
23 Mechanic Street
Girard, PA 16417

Cover design by Zachary Wincik

All photos by Stephanie Wincik unless otherwise indicated.

TABLE OF CONTENTS

Introduction..................................4

The Battles Museums....................7

Dead Man's Creek........................15

Pop...17

Lois..23

Gravity Hill..................................26

Beth's Hearts and Flowers..............29

Boom Town..................................32

Saucers..36

Premonitions................................40

Ouija..46

More Saucers 52

Spirit Photography........................55

The Eagle Hotel............................61

INTRODUCTION

No doubt about it, Erie County, Pennsylvania residents are a hardy lot. As far back as 1792 when the county was first established, folks here had to deal not only with the long cold snowy winters but also with the constant threat of death at the hands of the Iroquois Indians who inhabited the region.

According to a 1992 article by Mike Hudson in the Corry Journal, the leaders of the Six Iroquois Nations met with representatives from the Commonwealth of Pennsylvania in 1792 to turn over the land that is now Erie County for about $2000 in cash and goods. Unfortunately, not all of the Native Americans were pleased with this deal and some continued their attacks on Erie County settlers for many years.

The land that is now Erie County was also claimed by four other states besides Pennsylvania, all of whom were interested in the natural port at Presque Isle. In the end, Pennsylvania was the winner, but only after paying the federal government more than $150,000 for the land.

Obviously our early ancestors fought long and hard for this land and the generations that followed struggled to keep it, gradually improving the quality of our lives and shaping the Erie County we know today. Is it possible that after such a struggle some Erie County residents may be reluctant to leave, even after their earthly lives are over? We'll see.

In the pages of this book you will meet a diverse group of Erie Countians, some living in this world and some in the next. In the west county, paranormal investigators find evidence of spirits haunting a local museum. UFO sightings abound. Further south, a deranged woman still haunts the hotel she once tried to destroy.

Someone once asked me why there are so many ghost stories associated with Erie County. That's a good question, and one that I really can't answer well. I believe there are plenty of spirits everywhere, not just in Erie County, but one has to be "tuned in" in order to see or experience them. For reasons unknown to me, some people are able to "tune in" easily to paranormal phenomena, while most of us cannot.

Scientists are just now beginning to discover that all human beings operate on a certain "vibrational" level, and some people seem to vibrate at a higher frequency than others. Consider your car radio for a second. Naturally, you would not expect to hear your favorite station playing while your radio was tuned to a different station. Likewise, I suppose we cannot expect to see ghosts, or even

UFOs, if we don't happen to be operating on the same frequency as they are at the time.

Many of the individuals I interviewed for this book prefaced their story by saying, "You'll probably think I'm crazy." Sadly, paranormal experiences are often ridiculed in our western culture. This is not the case, however, in many other parts of the world. I recently watched a television documentary set in Iceland. Politicians, educators, physicians, philosophers, and police officers were interviewed, along with a number of "ordinary" citizens, about their experiences with what they refer to as "the hidden people." All of these individuals freely admitted to having regularly seen elves, fairies, and other creatures that most of us believe only exist in stories. The people of Iceland believe that due to their unique location on the earth, the energy there is "pure," allowing them to see what others cannot.

Crazy? Maybe. On the other hand, if you take a look back at the history of the world so far, I'll bet you can think of a few other folks who were once thought by their peers to be "crazy."

Galileo, Columbus, Pasteur, Einstein...

The Yellow House

THE BATTLES MUSEUMS

In 1858, lawyer-banker-farmer Rush Battles set about building a home on the outskirts of the tiny village of Girard, Pennsylvania. Rush's father had recently died, leaving him with the responsibility of providing a dwelling for his mother and two unmarried sisters. The home on Walnut Street, now commonly known as "the Yellow House" by the local residents, took two years to finish but the result was worth the wait. Much more elaborate than the typical Girard farmhouse of the time, the Italianate-style showplace was the talk of the town.

Since the home was spacious enough for more than one family, Rush also intended to live there along with his future bride when the time came for him to be married. Unfortunately, that day never arrived. Rush married Charlotte Webster, a headstrong and progressive young woman from a prominent Girard family, but just prior to their wedding day Charlotte announced that she had no intention of living with her future mother-in-law and wanted to have a home of her own. So in 1861 Rush began again and constructed a second, much smaller, home only a few hundred yards north of the first one.

After their honeymoon, Rush and Charlotte settled into their cozy farmhouse (dubbed "the White House" by today's Girardites) and started a family. Although the couple produced three children, only one survived the often-fatal childhood diseases of the nineteenth century to live to adulthood. Charlotte Elizabeth Battles, or "Beth" as she came to be called, was born in 1864 in the "White House" and would live there until her death in 1952.

Beth Battles grew to be a beautiful, intelligent and gracious young lady. Well-educated for a woman of her time, she attended both the Lake Erie Seminary in Painesville, Ohio and Mount Vernon Seminary in Washington, D.C.. There she met and married Charles Barber, an attorney, and the pair began their new life in the nation's capital. Within a few months, however, Rush Battles had traveled to Washington, retrieved his daughter and annulled the marriage. The reason for the breakup was never clear, although if the local gossip is to be believed, Barber revealed his true nature as an abusive scoundrel shortly after the couple's move from Girard.

Whatever the circumstances, it was apparently enough to sour Beth on the idea of marriage. She returned to her parent's home and poured her considerable energy into learning her father's business, developing her talent as an artist, and serving the Girard community. An active member of dozens of civic organizations, Beth Battles also served on the school board, and after her father's death became one of the nation's first female bank presidents.

By the 1920s, both of Beth's parents, as well as her grandmother and aunts, had died. On her own for the first time in her life, Beth found staying in the house by herself to be unbearably lonely and so invited a friend, Georgianna Read, to move in with her. The two women got along very well and together they remodeled the house, adding hardwood floors, two state-of-the-art bathrooms, and an extra bedroom on the second floor. Georgianna also had a talent for business and helped Beth to manage her father's many investments along with maintaining the Yellow House and the adjoining farmland.

For the next thirty years, the Battles estate thrived under the supervision of the two ladies. In addition to their many responsibilities, Beth and Georgianna found time to travel extensively as well as to entertain friends and business associates with elegant garden parties and teas. Despite their divergent personalities, Beth being quiet and soft-spoken while Georgianna a bit more tart, both women earned the love and respect of the Girard community.

In 1952, at the age of 88, Beth Battles passed away at her beloved White House on Walnut Street. Georgianna remained in the house for another thirty years, keeping up the Battles estate and carrying on business as usual until her own death at 100 years of age.

Upon the deaths of Miss Battles and Miss Read, the two Battles homes along with the surrounding property were willed to the Erie County Historical Society, and in the late 1980s were converted to the Battles Museums of Rural Life. The Yellow House is currently interpreted as a nineteenth century farmhouse, while the White House displays a multitude of furnishings, dishes, glassware, and other household items and heirlooms including two antique automobiles, all original possessions of the Battles family spanning more than two centuries.

Almost immediately after work was underway to renovate the century-old homes to allow for public visitation, the museum staff began to report unexplained incidents. Carefully placed items would disappear, only to be found somewhere else the next day. A plumber, working alone (or so he thought) in the upstairs bathroom of the White House one morning, was startled to suddenly see an elderly white-haired woman standing in the doorway. He spoke to her but receiving no reply, returned to his work. When he glanced up again the woman had vanished. Puzzled, the plumber walked next door to the Yellow House where staff was working on a photo exhibit of the Battles family, and mentioned that an old woman had been watching him work on the White House bathroom.

The White House

As he described the woman, his eyes fell on one particular photograph in the exhibit.

"That's her," he exclaimed. "That's the lady I saw. Who is she?"

"Georgianna Read," answered the astounded staff.

In the fifteen or so years since the Battles homes were opened as museums, ghostly occurrences have continued on a regular basis.

Visitors to the White House have reported feeling an invisible hand touch their arm or tug on their jacket as they wander through the first floor. Two volunteer tour guides, both self-professed skeptics, refuse to enter a second floor bedroom since being blasted with a gust of icy air while escorting visitors into the room during a recent evening tour.

The Yellow House has also had more than its share of reports of paranormal activity. The sound of children laughing and singing has been heard when no children were present in the house or on the grounds. Footsteps are frequently heard on the stairs and moving back and forth across the second floor when all of the staff is on the first floor. Lamps mysteriously change location by themselves. A woman visiting the house for a meeting left abruptly after insisting she saw a murky black figure looming in the doorway of the dining room. In one particularly startling incident, museum staff observed a full apparition of a woman clothed in a long black Victorian-style dress in an upstairs bedroom. The woman "floated" across the foot of the bed, then passed through the closed closet door and disappeared.

Shortly after the ghostly appearance in the bedroom, a group of paranormal investigators visited the Yellow House accompanied by a psychic who had no previous knowledge of the house's history. Various pieces of equipment were utilized by the investigators to determine if any correlation could be found between the electromagnetic energy in the house and the unusual events that had been witnessed by the staff. Very little out of the ordinary could be found on the first floor, however a sharp distortion of electromagnetic energy was discovered in the second floor bedroom near the closet door where the full apparition had been seen. The psychic also reported a strong impression of a female near the same closet door.

The paranormal findings would seem to make sense, considering that the house was occupied for many years by three females, Rush Battles' mother Elizabeth and his two sisters, Alcina and Lucina. Since all three lived in the home for most of their adult lives, certainly one can imagine any one of them feeling strongly enough about their home to stick around and make sure that all is in order. Perhaps they are even enjoying the energy brought about by the steady stream of visitors admiring their grand house.

So, if you happen to visit northwestern Erie County, stop in and visit the Battles Museums. More than likely, someone from the Battles family will be home!

DEAD MAN'S CREEK

Some folks in the west county area believe that not only are the Battles homes haunted, but the surrounding property may be affected as well. The story of Dead Man's Creek would seem to illustrate this point.

In the mid-nineteenth century, when the Battles family lived on the outskirts of Girard Borough and worked their prosperous farm, it was their custom to invite the entire town to a picnic on their property each summer. It was during one such summer picnic in 1861 that the legend of Dead Man's Creek was born.

After all had finished enjoying the bountiful food and drink, some of the men decided to walk off their meal by strolling along what was then known as Battles Creek. Battles Creek flows from an artesian spring under the ground and as a result seems almost to appear out of nowhere. As two of the men approached the creek, they made a disturbing discovery. Floating face down in the shallow water was the body of a young man in his early 20s. The man had obviously been murdered, his throat slashed from ear to ear.

The two men pulled the body from the creek, and their calls for help brought most of the townspeople running to see what had happened. Nobody recognized the young man, and no identification could be found on his body. For weeks, local authorities attempted to solve the case, to no avail.

On the surface, this story may seem to be just another unsolved killing. However, this case had a surprising twist. When the body was found, the young man was dressed in a brand new, perfectly fitting uniform from the War of 1812.

Local residents have developed a number of theories to explain this strange event, none of which of course can be proven. A suicide? Possibly, but not likely considering how the man was killed. A simple murder in which the killer or killers dressed the man in the uniform as some sort of twisted joke or in an attempt to throw off the authorities? Maybe. Or, one of the more intriguing explanations- is it possible that the Battles property contains a "hole in time" through which this man from 1812 suddenly appeared nearly fifty years after his death?

POP

Many times when hauntings occur, the person being haunted has no clue as to the identity of the spirit. Some people, however, have the good fortune (or in some cases, the misfortune) of knowing precisely who the spirit is who is making their presence known. So it is with Carl and Susan Sanders. Both believe it is Susan's father who is haunting their home, and they consider it a gift.

Carl and Susan told me their story as we sat in the kitchen of their quiet comfortable home outside of Edinboro, Pennsylvania, one snowy morning last winter. Carl, a former police officer with a direct, matter-of-fact manner, came straight to the point. "I'm not going to try to convince you of anything," he began. "I don't care if you believe me or not." That aside, Carl went on to describe the unusual occurrences that have led him and his wife to believe that their house is haunted.

Carl and Susan built their home in the late 1980s, and Susan's father lived next door. Carl was very close to his father-in-law, or "Pop" as he calls him, noting that he had not had the opportunity to get to know his own father very well, which made his relationship with Pop even more precious. After

Pop died, a series of unexplained events began to occur, convincing Carl that his father-in-law's spirit was still with him.

One evening about nine o'clock, Carl was sitting in the living room watching television after Susan had gone to bed. Out of nowhere, Carl suddenly felt "a tunnel of cold air" blowing on his left cheek. Carl knew instinctively that it was Pop, just trying to get his attention. Another evening at about the same time, Carl was again watching television when he distinctly heard footsteps that began in the hallway, crossed through the living room and moved into the kitchen. Thinking it was Susan, Carl called out to her but she didn't answer. When Carl got up to investigate, he found he was alone in the room and Susan was still in bed, sound asleep.

Carl has also sensed what he calls "an energy field" of some kind that he actually bumps up against from time to time, once while looking out of the front window, and on more than one occasion while in his basement workshop.

Fairly recently, an incident occurred which Carl says "shook me in my boots." Sitting at the kitchen table one evening, Carl looked up to see a full-body apparition of Pop standing near the kitchen doorway. The image lasted only a few seconds, Carl remembers, but was so clear that Carl could even make out the red plaid shirt Pop was wearing. The spirit did not move or speak, but simply faded away.

Susan also believes that her father is there and that he uses various electrical appliances to make himself known. The television frequently turns off by itself, she says. On at least two occasions when Susan and Carl were out for the evening, they returned to find lights turned on that they knew had been off when they left. A teardrop lamp sometimes moves on its own, without any visible cause.

After Carl and Susan had described to me the numerous events they have witnessed on the first floor of their home, Carl took me to the basement, explaining that Pop seems to enjoy hanging out there even more. It's no wonder. Carl's workshop is filled with enough tools and equipment to rival a small hardware store, and is even better organized. Row after row of tiny drawers filled with nuts and bolts line the walls, all meticulously sorted and labeled. Every item has its place, and it is obvious that Carl would know immediately if anything was not in its correct location. It is here that Pop seems to like playing practical jokes on his son-in-law.

Displacement of tools that Carl is working with is a fairly frequent occurrence. Working alone at the counter repairing an antique clock one afternoon, Carl laid his screwdriver down to answer the phone. When he came back downstairs a few moments later, the screwdriver had been moved approximately five feet to the other end of the counter.

Counter in Carl's workshop

A collector of unique antiques as well as tools, Carl showed me a small hand-held time clock he had acquired, which was about the size of a large rubber stamp. Normally, he explained, the clock hangs on the wall face out. On at least two occasions, Carl has entered his workshop to find the time clock turned around with its face against the wall. A CB radio antenna that had been hanging securely on the wall behind some water pipes abruptly fell one day, landing several feet across the room.

A few days after our first meeting, Carl called to tell me of another puzzling event that had just occurred in his workshop. Carl explained that he had removed a drill bit from its usual space on the wall and took it upstairs to use in the kitchen. When he returned to the basement to put the bit away, a black nail was hanging in its place. According to Carl, he owns no nails of that size or color. He took the nail from the wall, placed it on the top shelf of a small freestanding cabinet and locked the cabinet door. A short time later, when Carl returned with a friend to show him what had happened, the nail had vanished. After an extensive search of the workshop by the two men, the "traveling nail" was finally found inside one of the cabinet drawers.

Cabinet holding the "traveling nail"

Even though some of Pop's "tricks" can sometimes be disconcerting, Carl and Susan are not frightened by them, in fact just the opposite is true. "None of the occurrences in this house would lead us to believe he is trying to upset us," Carl says, and goes on to say that he feels blessed by Pop's presence. "It's like a treasure to me."

LOIS

Like so many other folks who have had a paranormal experience, Lois Bartos prefaces her story with, "People think I'm strange." Lois is one of those rare individuals with the ability to peer into another world that most of us cannot see.

One of Lois's first experiences with the spirit world occurred when she was much younger and living on West 11th Street in Erie. The ghost of a man dressed in a plaid jacket and who appeared to have no legs would materialize in Lois's bedroom on a regular basis. The man never spoke, nor did he seem to want anything of her other than to make his presence known.

Later, after Lois and her husband moved into a house on Perry Street, a number of strange occurrences began to befall Lois while her husband inexplicably was not affected. Lois believes this is because her husband's first wife, now deceased, resents her and enjoys being able to annoy Lois from her place on the other side. Household items Lois is using mysteriously vanish, and then suddenly reappear elsewhere. Loud pounding can be heard within the walls, then ceases when Lois's husband enters the room. Once, the bathroom shower unexpectedly turned itself on and soaked

Lois's newly styled hair. While preparing to attend a party one day, Lois was dumfounded to see the twist tie on a bag of powdered sugar in her kitchen unravel itself and blow sugar all over her black suit.

The most startling event occurred when Lois was letting the dog outside and witnessed a full apparition of a woman in "pearlescent white" glowing in front of her.

Shortly afterward, Lois and her husband decided to move to a new home on Melrose Avenue. For a while, Lois noticed no unusual activity in the house and was starting to believe that her problems with spirits were over. Recently, however, Lois has begun to experience the signs of a haunting once again. Boxes filled with holiday decorations that were securely stored on shelves in the garage fell to the floor without warning, breaking all of the ornaments inside. Downstairs in the "rec room" of her new home, Lois's dogs will suddenly begin to growl while staring up at a corner of the room, the hair on their backs standing on end. And once while descending the stairs to the rec room, Lois felt a hand trying to push her the rest of the way.

Is it possible that some spirits prefer to haunt a family or an individual rather than remaining attached to a single location? To Lois it would seem so. Hopefully at some point Lois will find a way to help this apparently unhappy spirit find its way back home.

GRAVITY HILL

Just a few miles southwest of North East Borough lies a mysterious stretch of road known as Gravity Hill. Located on Moorheadville Road at the top of the I-90 overpass, Gravity Hill, or "Spook Hill," as it is sometimes called, is best known as a place where objects, including your vehicle, can actually roll uphill.

According to information provided by the International Directory of Magnetic Hills, Gravity Hills, Mystery Hills, and Magnetic Mountains, sites such as Gravity Hill can be found all across the United States and even around the world. Many have speculated that the effect is due to abnormalities in the earth's magnetic or gravitational fields, and some even attribute the anomaly to the unseen spirits of long-dead Native Americans who reportedly still haunt the area.

But, unlike most of the paranormal phenomena discussed in this book, North East's Gravity Hill and others like it can be explained by modern science as a simple optical illusion. Sites such as Gravity Hill are generally found in areas where the actual horizon is obscured. Trees, walls, or other structures that help us to visually decide what is vertical may be leaning slightly, and if the horizon cannot be seen our eyes can be tricked by objects that we expect to be vertical but which really are not. This creates the illusion that a downhill slope is actually an uphill one, especially if the slope is not steep.

Even so, when you visit Gravity Hill it is very difficult to believe that the experience is only an illusion. Sitting with your car in neutral, the sensation is one of being pulled steadily uphill by an invisible magnet. As much as one tries to see the uphill slope as a downhill one, it's still easier (and more fun) to imagine that unexplained forces are at work on Gravity Hill. In the face of overwhelming evidence to the contrary, though, I guess we have to give science this one.

Gravity Hill
Photo by Zachary Wincik

BETH'S HEARTS AND FLOWERS

If you drive through downtown Girard, Pennsylvania, you will immediately be struck by the historic appearance of this quaint little town. Established in 1846 at the crossroads of Route 20 and what was then the Erie Canal Extension, Girard has retained its small-town atmosphere for more than 150 years.

Many of the buildings along Girard's beautiful tree-lined Main Street are the original structures that formerly housed cabinetmakers, blacksmiths, grocers, hatters, and innkeepers during the nineteenth century. Our ghost story takes place in a charming little flower shop located on the south side of Main Street, nestled between the drugstore and a barbershop complete with an old-fashioned barber pole. "Beth's Hearts and Flowers" is owned and operated by Nancy Briody and her daughter Beth, however it appears that someone else may also be lending a hand around the shop from time to time.

When the previous owner of the shop alluded to her that "things move around sometimes," Nancy passed it off as just something that happens in old buildings. Before long, though, Nancy began to have some strange experiences of her own. Tools and other small items would vanish, then reappear later in anther room. Objects would tip over or fall to the floor for no apparent reason. Once, when Nancy was talking about these unexplained events with a group of Beth's friends, the girls were shocked to see a single keychain from a display rack containing multiple keychains inexplicably fall to the floor in front of them.

One day when Nancy was working alone in the shop, she suddenly had the feeling that someone else was in the room with her. She looked up in time to see a man dressed in a white shirt, dark suit, and a "1940s-style" hat walking across the room in front of her. Although Nancy could see the man clearly, she describes him as "not solid" and could tell "he was not a real person."

Nevertheless, the man who I will call "Bill" was certainly real at some point. In the 1940s, the two story building in which the flower shop is now located was divided into apartments. Bill reportedly lived in the first floor apartment near the front of the building. When Bill was not seen around town for a week or so, a few of the townsfolk decided to investigate. Upon entering his apartment they found Bill in his bedroom, apparently dead for several days.

Nancy believes it is Bill's spirit that still lingers in the flower shop, and both she and her daughter Beth have seen his apparition on a number of occasions. He seems to be more active, Nancy says, when the furniture in the shop is moved around to make way for changing displays. Beth reports that he seems particularly concerned with the location of a certain antique washstand. Any time the washstand is moved, she notes that the bar on the back of the stand is taken down every morning, several days in a row.

Both Nancy and Beth find Bill's presence not particularly frightening but "a little spooky," and sometimes just plain annoying. When his shenanigans get out of hand, Nancy has found that "if I yell at him he will stop," sometimes for weeks at a time. The down side of this, she says, is that whenever Bill is not in the flower shop, it's a safe bet that the gentleman renting the upstairs apartment will begin to complain of similar problems and will send Bill back downstairs.

Nancy notes that there is definitely one good thing about having Bill around. The bedroom in which Bill died is situated in the rear of the shop, just off Nancy's workroom. Summer and winter, and without the benefit of air conditioning, the temperature in that room remains ice cold, allowing Nancy's flowers stay cool and fresh, courtesy of Bill.

BOOM TOWN

Corry, Pennsylvania, is a delightful city rich in history. Situated in the southeastern corner of Erie County, Corry had its beginnings well before the start of the Civil War, when wealthy landowner Hiram Corry decided to sell a piece of his property to the railroad. Because of this particular railroad stop's proximity to the Titusville oil fields in nearby Crawford County, Corry became the ideal location for the world's first commercial oil refinery, the Downer and Kent Oil Works.

Along with the refinery came an inevitable increase in population; by 1863 Corry was large enough to call itself a borough, and with the continuing oil boom it soon grew to become the City of Corry by 1866. At one point in the 1880s, Corry was jokingly dubbed "The City of Stumps" because the city's growth was faster than the removal of the stumps left from clearing the surrounding forest.

In Corry's early days, more than one well-known personality had ties to the city. Mark Twain often visited his mother and brother who lived on Washington Street, and New York City newspaper founder and ardent abolitionist Horace Greeley dropped in on his father's Wayne Township farm from time to time.

Fast forward 150 years, and we find the Corry of today a modern city that still manages to retain its old-fashioned charm. As is the case in many older communities, Corry's streets are lined with both vintage buildings and newer establishments. Our ghost story takes place in the early 1970s, in one such older home on 2nd Avenue.

Joni Giacoma Chadwell was born in Corry in 1960 and lived in the house on 2nd Avenue until she was in the sixth grade. An elderly couple had previously lived there, and Joni believes that the husband had passed away inside the house. Although her early childhood in the house was uneventful, shortly before her family's planned move to a new home Joni began to experience some unexplained occurrences.

On more than one occasion while playing in her bedroom during the day, Joni witnessed a black shadow floating eerily across the wall. The shadow had no particular form and always faded away when it reached her closet door. At other times, the little girl could see nothing, but could feel a chill spread through the room accompanied by the unmistakable sensation that someone was watching her.

When Joni was about twelve years old, she began to receive regular and terrifying nighttime visits from a malevolent spirit who would appear to her in her bedroom several times a week. Joni remembers that the visitor had a "cold, gray presence about him," and she could feel him hovering over her as she lay in her bed. As Joni recalls, the entity would speak to her, repeatedly warning her not to scream for her mother while at the same time pinching her arms, legs, or any part of her body that happened to be above the covers. Paralyzed with fright, the child was unable to move or make a sound. Sometimes, as she recalls, Joni was able to muster enough courage to scream for her mother. As soon as she did so, however, the man dissolved into a vapor and "misted away" just as her mother got to the room.

    As might be expected, Joni's mother did not believe her story, dismissing it as simply a child's recurring nightmare. Fortunately, not long after Joni's ordeal began, the family moved to their new home and the issue was resolved. To Joni's relief the spirit did not attempt to follow her as she had feared he might.

    More than thirty years later, Joni still remembers the ghostly events of her childhood clearly and is adamant that she was not dreaming them as her mother suspected. So, who was the negative entity that terrorized Joni, and what could have caused the spirit to be so angry that he vented his rage upon an innocent child? The answer is anyone's guess, but certainly in a town as old as

Corry there are bound to be a few unpleasant spirits mixed in with the gentle ones. Joni reports that the home was demolished several years after her family's move and is now the site of the Corry Community Center; to her knowledge there have been no reports of spirit activity at the Center, so hopefully the spirit who haunted Joni has moved on to a happier place.

SAUCERS

I've known Dave Shaffer since I was a little girl. A well-known and respected citizen of Girard Borough in western Erie County, Dave is retired from his job as a hospital radiology technician but remains active in the church and in a number of local civic organizations. Whether he is building an exhibit for the local museum, attending a borough zoning meeting, or pruning his exquisite gardens, Dave is the kind of guy who knows everyone in town, is always busy but still finds time to do more, and is always willing to lend a hand wherever it's needed. Dave also has a wealth of information about Girard history stored in his head, along with a talent for storytelling that can make even the most mundane event come alive. The story you're about to read, however, is anything but mundane.

One warm summer night in 1957, it was business as usual for Dave as he wrapped up his second shift duties at the Model Works factory in Girard. Back then, Dave worked one of his first jobs on a line making railroad tracks. At the end of the evening one of his responsibilities was to close the large ventilation windows located high above the shop floor, so every night at eleven-thirty he climbed a ladder to the catwalk and systematically moved around the perimeter of the building until all of the windows were secured. It was during one of these routine walks that Dave experienced an event he can still recall vividly, almost fifty years after it happened.

"I was just going along," Dave remembers, "and then I heard the sound of like a diesel engine to a locomotive. I thought maybe they were out back loading some of the railroad cars. I looked down to see if I could see an engine, and as I raised my head back up I saw three flying saucers just as clear as a bell. I couldn't believe my eyes. They were just above the roof, about 20 or 25 yards from me." Dave pointed to a drawing he made of the crafts. "Those squares, the windows along the bottom, were jet black in color. The whole thing glowed, but had no lights. The best way I can describe it is if you turned an aluminum pan upside down and shone a flashlight on it."

The crafts did not spin or rotate, Dave recalls, and all three appeared to be the same size. They also were not interested in sticking around after their presence was discovered. "As soon as my eyes made contact with them they started moving away from me in perfect formation. They all moved together simultaneously. The noise lessened as they got farther away from me and of course I realized then that the sound wasn't from a locomotive."

After the saucers disappeared, "I finished closing the windows," Dave says, "but I came down that ladder shaking like a leaf and had to sit down in a chair." When a co-worker approached him and asked what was wrong, Dave related the story to him and the shift supervisor, but then "nothing more was ever said about it."

Later, Dave did tell the story to his mother and his wife, but like many who have had similar experiences he told no one else for many years, worried that "people would probably think I was nuts."

Not a chance, Dave.

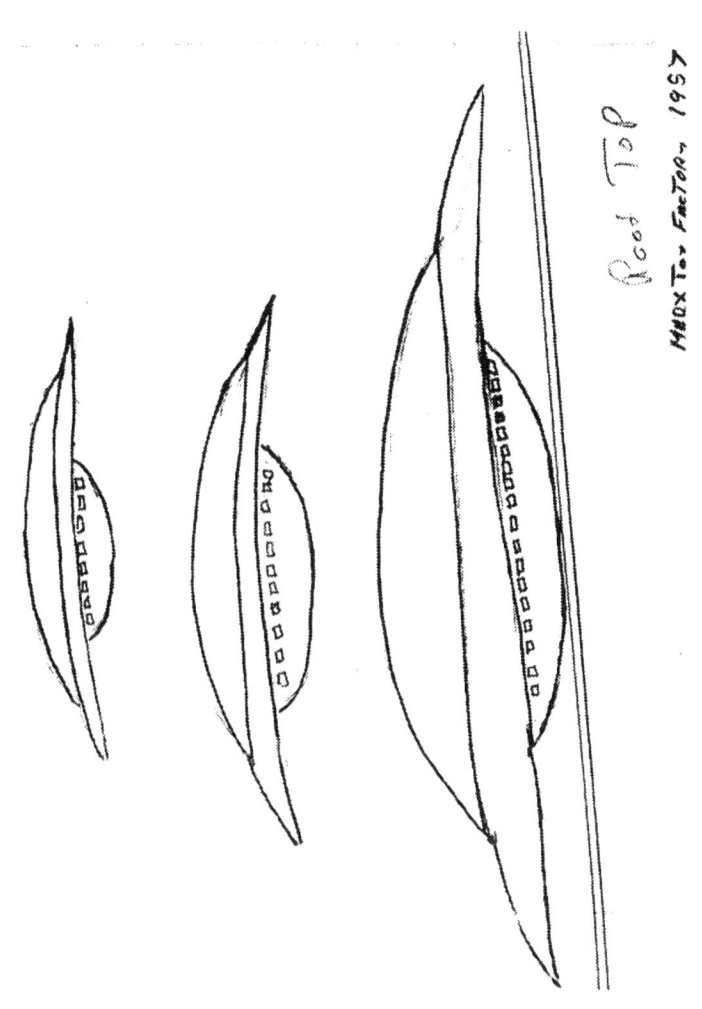

Drawing by Dave Shaffer

PREMONITIONS

Often stories of the paranormal tend to raise more questions than answers about the possibility of life on other planes of existence and our ability as humans to become aware of those alternate planes. Such is the case with Union City native Karen Luma.

Karen has had experiences she cannot explain since she was very young. Karen's grandmother, with whom she was not particularly close, died when Karen was thirteen years old. Karen explains that her grandmother was of a generation and culture who believed that children "should be seen and not heard," so much so that Karen cannot recall her grandmother ever speaking directly to her. Shortly after her grandmother's death, Karen awoke suddenly in the middle of the night, certain she could hear her name being called. She opened her eyes to see her grandmother standing at the foot of her bed. "I want you to tell everyone I am fine and not to worry," her grandmother said, then faded back into a very bright light and was gone.

The next morning, Karen told her parents what had happened. Although her mother dismissed the experience as simply a dream, Karen's father told her that this type of occurrence was quite common on his side of the family and he believed it probably happened just as Karen described.

A similar encounter with a ghost occurred a few years later when Karen was eighteen. Karen's Aunt Jenny, a double amputee, had recently died from complications related to diabetes. Shortly after Aunt Jenny's funeral, Karen was driving to work at about eight o'clock in the morning. She was alone on the road and had stopped at a traffic light. As she waited for the light to change, Karen happened to glance off to her left. There was Aunt Jenny in front of the pharmacy, standing tall and "all dressed up, looking like she was waiting for the bus." Karen could not believe her eyes. She looked back at the traffic light and then back at Aunt Jenny, but she had vanished.

A year or so later, Karen was visiting a friend's house. The girls were chatting and listening to records when Karen suddenly had a very strong premonition that her boyfriend (and future husband,) Ken, had been involved in a traffic accident in which the vehicle he was in had rolled over. Karen was unable to shake the ominous feeling, and since she had not seen Ken for a few days decided to contact his friends to find out where he was. When she finally reached his best friend, she was told that not Ken, but Ken's brother, had indeed been involved in a rollover crash the night before.

    Years passed, and Karen and Ken eventually married. In the spring of 1970 when the pair was expecting their second child, they bought a nine-acre farm and happily settled down to raise their family. All was well until the fall of that same year. Shortly after the child was born, Karen began to experience a series of eerie, unexplained events. "Every day for weeks," she says, "I would hear a woman's voice that sounded just like my mother, screaming my name. I would fly outside, thinking she had come to visit and maybe had fallen, and there would be nobody there. This happened day after day, until I really thought I was losing my mind." Karen also noticed that during this time the family dog followed her everywhere, so close that she tripped over him at every turn.

    Then, one day Karen and her husband were preparing to go on a trip to visit some friends. Karen remembers that although Ken was usually helpful with getting the children ready and packing the car, on this particular day "he just sat in a chair and did nothing." Irritated, Karen asked him to get up and help her. "He just looked at me," Karen recalls, "and then he told me that I'd better get used to doing this by myself. After that he just got up and left the room." Although she tried to brush off the remark, Karen worried that Ken was no longer happy with their marriage and wanted to get out of it.

    The next morning, Ken got up to go to work as usual, but "when I kissed him goodbye that morning," Karen remembers, "I knew in my heart that I would never see him again. I couldn't call him back; it was like I had no voice. I just watched him get into his vehicle and drive off to work. A few hours later, I got a phone call that he had been putting an elbow in a manhole in a fourteen-foot ditch and the entire ditch caved in on him and killed him. It was a horrific end to a very bizarre few weeks."

    Some time later, Karen and a friend decided to take the children to a park not far from Karen's home. A shallow creek ran through the area and the children enjoyed fishing for crawdads and picnicking by the water. The park was "pretty rustic" at the time, Karen says, with only a few other families there. As Karen and her friend watched the children play, "all of a sudden this 1953 Chevy drove past" on the road nearby. Karen remembers that the car "had a different type of paint job and paraphernalia on it. There were two gentlemen in the car that I couldn't see clearly. The car stopped just beyond us, and the passenger got out and walked around to the driver's side."

    At this point, Karen and her friend looked at each other. "That guy walks just like your Ken," her friend said, and Karen agreed. As the two women continued to observe the car and its occupants, they noticed that the paint and other markings on the car seemed familiar. Then they remembered. A friend they had known in high school, Terry Moore, had owned a car exactly like the one they were seeing now. Terry had been killed in an auto accident when the girls were in eleventh grade. As Karen and her friend tried to absorb this information, "all of a sudden out of nowhere, a girl appeared and walked up to the car," Karen says. "My friend and I looked at each other, and when we looked back everything was gone, the car, the people, everything."

Thinking about Karen's experiences brings a number of questions to mind. Were Karen and her friend watching a rerun of a scene from the past? Is it possible that tiny tears in the fabric of space and time can sometimes occur, allowing us to get a glimpse of another dimension? Why do some human beings have the ability to see the future and not others? And for those who do experience premonitions of the future, why does this occur intermittently and not all the time? Does psychic ability run in families, as Karen's father seemed to believe? Hopefully as the human race progresses, we will become more comfortable discussing these fascinating questions, and both the scientific community and the general population will become more willing to accept parapsychology as a serious field of study. When that happens, perhaps much of what we consider now to be mysterious will become clear.

OUIJA

The first Ouija boards appeared in the United States in the late 1880s and were extremely popular during the Victorian era. According to Robert Todd Carroll, author of "The Skeptic's Dictionary," the board was named "Ouija" after the Egyptian word for good luck. Although Ouija is not really Egyptian for good luck, Charles Kennard, one of the developers of the modern version of the game, reported that the board told him it was, so the name stuck.

For those not familiar with the Ouija board, the game consists of a piece of cardboard upon which the letters of the alphabet are printed along with the words "yes," "no," "maybe," and "goodbye," and a planchette, a plastic 3-legged device used for pointing. Players ask the board a question while touching the planchette lightly with their fingertips. The planchette then slides across the board (supposedly powered by psychokinetic forces,) pointing toward the letters and words until the answer to the user's question is spelled out.

Believers in the Ouija board insist that supernatural forces help to spell out the answers, while others believe that the users themselves either consciously or unconsciously move the planchette to obtain the answers they desire. Probably few of us grew to adulthood without dabbling with a Ouija board at least once, and the two young men who told me about their paranormal experiences are no exception.

Jason Gibbs and Eric Perrye have been best friends since the fourth grade. Growing up together in northwestern Erie County, the two had much in common, sharing camping trips, fishing excursions, roller coaster rides and sleepovers. In addition to these fun-filled pursuits, the two have also shared some darker experiences. Both seem to be sensitive to paranormal phenomena, and both have had a run-in with a Ouija board.

Jason's childhood home was built in the 1800s and had reportedly been used at one time as a station on the Underground Railroad. Over the years, Jason recalls a number of unexplained events that have occurred in his home. A rocking chair frequently rocks by itself. The pungent odor of cherry pipe tobacco wafts through the house from time to time, even though the only family member ever to smoke a pipe was Jason's deceased grandfather. The family dog, Sam, often paces through the house, the hair on his back standing up as he barks and growls at "nothing."

One evening while Jason was relaxing on his couch in the living room, the television turned on by itself. Puzzled, he got up and turned it off, then returned to the couch. Seconds later, the television snapped on again. Once more Jason got up and switched it off, only to have it come back on the moment he sat down. This time, Jason decided to stand beside the television to see what would happen. He discovered that as long as he stayed beside the television it would remain off, but the moment he ventured back to his place on the couch, the mischievous spirit flipped it on again.

Eric tells of visiting Jason at his home one evening. The hour was late when the two had finished talking, so Eric decided to spend the night rather than drive home. Asleep on a futon in the second floor computer room, Eric suddenly woke around two-thirty in the morning to find the computer keyboard typing furiously by itself. The computer was turned off at the time, and no living typist was in sight. Needless to say, Eric slept downstairs the remainder of the night.

Eric is no stranger to spooky experiences, as the house in which he grew up apparently harbors some spirits of its own. A common thread that runs through many supernatural tales is the fascination that spirits seem to have with manipulating electrical appliances, and this appears to be the case with an impish entity who once terrified Eric and his older brother using a telephone.

When he was about twelve years old, Eric and his seventeen-year-old brother were home alone

one afternoon when his brother attempted to make a phone call. He was prevented from doing so, however, by a series of loud noises that suddenly began emanating from the speakerphone. "We kept hearing the same sounds over and over," Eric recalls. The high-pitched cry of an infant. Heavy footsteps walking back and forth over a creaky floor. The repeated pounding of a metal hammer. "My brother turned the speaker phone off. It was scary—terrifying. We turned the phone off three times but the sounds were still there. My brother sent me to check the other phones in the house and they were all hung up."

Eric remembers running down the street and bringing a friend back to hear the strange noises. When they returned to the house, Eric recalls, all of them were shocked that the eerie sounds had not subsided. "We just sat there, not believing what we heard. The sounds were repeating themselves over and over, in no set pattern, sometimes faster, sometimes louder, then so quiet they were hard to make out. At one point, the sounds all mixed together at the same time." After about twenty minutes, the noises stopped as abruptly as they had started and never returned. This experience, along with several other unexplained occurrences such as the sound of heavy breathing regularly heard in his bedroom at night, was enough to convince Eric that there might be something other than living persons residing in his house.

And then there was that thing with the Ouija board. Like his friend Jason, Eric was never quite sure he believed all of the superstitions surrounding Ouija boards. True, they were fun to play with, but certainly they couldn't be taken seriously. Jason changed his mind one night when he decided to challenge the board. "If you're real," he said aloud, "then make the phone ring." The phone rang, and there was no one there.

Not to be outdone by his friend, Eric had a startling Ouija tale of his own. Even though he had heard stories from others that a Ouija board can be difficult to dispose of (a friend told him of screams heard coming from a burn barrel when she was trying to burn an old Ouija game,) he wasn't sure he believed the tales. However, one day an incident occurred that made him wonder if there might not be a grain of truth in the legends.

As a youngster, Eric had borrowed a Ouija board from a friend in his neighborhood. After playing with it for a while, Eric grew tired of the game and left it sitting on the railing of his front porch. Early the next morning, Eric woke to the sound of a driving rainstorm. Remembering he had left the Ouija board outside, he leaped out of bed and ran to the porch, imagining how angry his friend was going to be when she found out her game was ruined. When he reached the porch and picked up the game, Eric's jaw dropped in amazement. Despite the pounding rain that had soaked everything around it, the Ouija board was completely dry, untouched by the storm.

MORE SAUCERS

Once known as Jackson's Cross Roads, Albion, Pennsylvania is the southernmost borough in Erie County. Much like nearby Girard, Albion sprang up along the banks of the Erie Canal Extension in the mid-1800s. Although the canal met its demise less than thirty years after its inception, the canal route was quickly replaced with railroad lines that helped the borough continue to flourish. Today, Albion maintains an active business district surrounded on all sides by sprawling farmhouses and lush fields.

Deb Perrye and her three sisters grew up in one such farmhouse just north of Albion on Route 215. Even though Albion may seem like a quiet location to some, for Deb and her siblings nothing could be further from the truth. In a telephone interview from her home in Florida, Deb recalls that her childhood home and even the surrounding woods and fields were a hotbed of paranormal activity in the mid-1960s.

Although neither Deb nor her sisters ever saw an actual apparition in their home, there were enough unusual occurrences to convince them that at the very least some type of poltergeist-like entity was at work there. Violin music without an apparent source could frequently be heard emanating from the dishes in the china cabinet. The image of a skeleton was seen dangling from a doorway, then disappeared. A young child visiting the house insisted he was chased down the hallway by a dressmaker's mannequin.

One night, Deb, her sisters, and several friends decided to hold a séance in the house. Using a Ouija board, the group intended to try to contact Deb's deceased father. They lit a candle and proceeded to ask the father to come through. With each question the girls asked, the candle flame flickered from side to side, which they interpreted as a "yes" response. When they asked if the father would like to speak with one of Deb's sisters, the flame "suddenly shot up to the ceiling." After this incident, the terrified teens ended the séance and the use of the Ouija board.

And as if the ghostly activity in her home was not enough to scare her out of her wits, Deb reports that she also had more than one close encounter with a UFO during the years she lived in Albion. Walking with a friend one night in the wooded area near her home, a "huge glowing light" suddenly appeared in the sky above them. The light shone brightly for a few seconds, then vanished as quickly as it had come. On another occasion near Cherry Hill Road, "a huge UFO flew past" Deb and three of her friends. Interestingly, Deb observed that their car stalled when the craft was near them, then started up again immediately after the object disappeared.

One of Deb's sisters also reports a UFO sighting, this one near "Jumbo Woods," just off Route 6N. The sighting occurred while she was on her way to work. The craft hovered for some time just above the tree line, and for a moment appeared to be following her before dropping out of sight.

Strangely enough, Deb's tale is only one of many UFO sightings reported in Erie County in the 1950s and 1960s. Why in this area, and why were the sightings so frequent during that time period? Of course, we can only speculate about the answers to these questions. If, as many believe, otherworldly beings are indeed observing us and systematically studying our civilization, perhaps Erie County was simply on their "to-do" list for those decades!

SPIRIT PHOTOGRAPHY

If you are looking for an authentic slice of Americana, you need look no further than picture-perfect North East, Pennsylvania. Located along the banks of Lake Erie just west of the New York-Pennsylvania state line, North East exemplifies the best of what small-town life has to offer. Incorporated in 1834, North East was the home of the first railroad line in Erie County. Perhaps most well-known for its magnificent grape vineyards and associated wineries, North East also boasts beautiful Gibson Park, a thriving Main Street, a local branch of Mercyhurst College, and a vast array of community organizations and activities. With a spring-to-fall Farmer's Market, a Fireman's Cherry Festival, Fourth of July fireworks, and even an annual Pumpkin Decorating Contest at Halloween, there is something for everyone all year round in North East. And, as in most older communities, there's also a ghost or two.

    Bob and Cindy Riefstahl moved into their lovely 150-year-old North East home in 1971. The house is situated in a pleasant residential neighborhood that was once known as "Little Italy" or "Little Brooklyn" by the immigrants who first settled there. Although they do not know who all of the previous owners of the house were, Bob and Cindy do know that at one point in the past their home was used as a boardinghouse. And although the couple has not experienced apparitions, displaced objects, or the eerie sensations often associated with a traditional haunting, they have reason to suspect that there is something out of the ordinary in their home.

Cindy recalls that shortly after she and Bob moved into the house, she suddenly and inexplicably developed a very strong interest in sewing. Even though she had never enjoyed sewing up to that point (in fact, she admits to being "very bad at it" in her high school home economics class) Cindy decided to begin making clothes for her children as a way to help out with the family budget. Bob purchased an old sewing machine for her to use, and before long she was so adept at the skill that she decided to take some classes to improve even further. Eventually, Cindy became a full-time seamstress/tailor and started her own successful home-based business. Many years later, she discovered during a conversation with Bob's grandmother, Marie, that a seamstress had formerly lived in Cindy's house and had operated a sewing business there. Marie remembered her mother bringing her to the house as a child when she needed to have some sewing done. Cindy believes it is possible that this spirit may have been responsible for influencing her career choice.

In 1990, another incident occurred in their home that Bob and Cindy are still unable to explain. It was Christmastime, and the Riefstahl's son had just received a small Kodak camera as one of his gifts. Excited, the youngster roamed through the house, randomly snapping photos of anything in his path. When the film was developed, Bob and Cindy made a startling discovery. A photo of their Christmas tree reveals the clear image of a man in a military uniform next to the tree, speaking with a woman in a large feathered hat. The couple is sure there was no window or television nearby to cause a reflection, and a professional photographer who later examined the photo declared it to be authentic.

Two other pictures on the same roll of film contained images that astounded the Riefstahls. In the first, the figures of a bride and groom can be seen outlined against a photo of the back door. The second picture is one of the family dog standing next to the kitchen table with an image of the Riefstahl's parakeet, Dagwood, reflected on the tabletop. The dog was alive and well at the time the photo was taken, but the unfortunate Dagwood had passed away almost 10 years before.

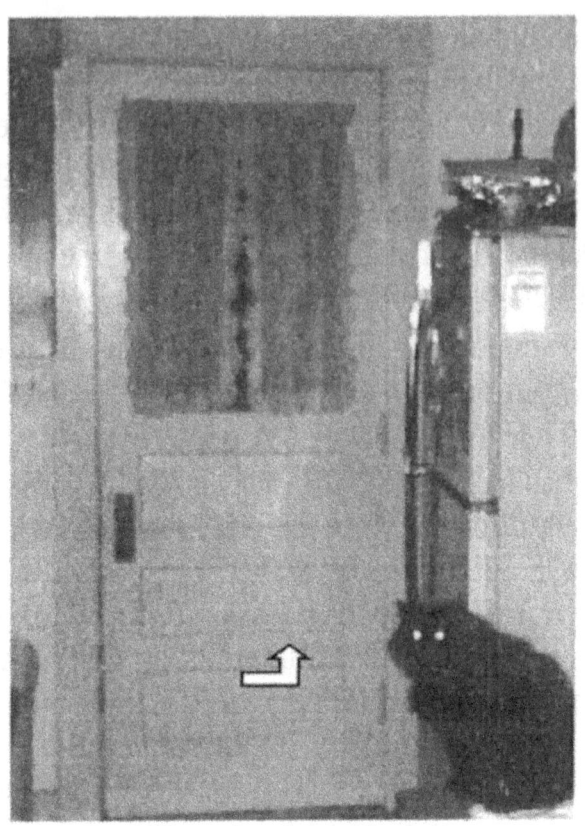
Back door bride and groom

In the years since the photos were taken, Bob and Cindy have tried unsuccessfully to discover the identity of the people in the pictures. "People sometimes think we're crazy," Cindy says. Even so, no one who has seen the photographs so far has been able to offer the Riefstahls a satisfactory explanation of how these unusual images found their way into ordinary family photos.

Once again, the Riefstahl's story raises more questions than answers about paranormal phenomena. Could the same leftover energy that might linger after death and produce a ghostly apparition, also make an imprint on a camera lens?

The Riefstahl's Christmas tree

Dagwood the parakeet

THE EAGLE HOTEL

Waterford, Pennsylvania, located in southern Erie County, is one town that can honestly say that "George Washington slept here." In 1753, when Waterford was held by the French and known as Fort LeBoeuf, a young George Washington traveled here on a mission for the governor of Virginia. He delivered a letter to the commander of Fort LeBoeuf, demanding that the French withdraw their forces from this region since it had been claimed by Great Britain. The mission was not immediately successful, however six years later the French finally withdrew and were replaced by British troops, then later by United States troops. By the early 1800s, Waterford had developed into a prosperous settlement and was incorporated as a borough in 1833.

The imposing Eagle Hotel has stood watch over the Waterford community for 180 years. Built by innkeeper Thomas King in 1826, the building was constructed out of stone from a local quarry and was originally used as a tavern. In the years since then the building has also served as a stagecoach stop, an office for a traveling dentist, a dance hall, and a fashionable hotel/resort.

As one might expect, the interior of the Eagle Hotel has undergone a multitude of changes between the year it was built and the present day. One such change occurred in the summer of 1845 when according to Waterford residents, "a deranged chambermaid" set fire to the establishment. Extensive repairs were required and it would be nearly a year before the building could be re-opened.

A long succession of proprietors followed, and then in the late 1970s the building was purchased by the Fort LeBoeuf Historical Society. The Society began an ongoing restoration project, and today the Eagle Hotel has almost been returned to its original appearance. The Hotel is currently being utilized as a restaurant featuring delicious home-style cooking.

It is mainly in the kitchen of this fine eatery that staff members have witnessed peculiar activity which some attribute to the ghost of "Matilda," the crazed employee who nearly destroyed the Eagle Hotel well over a century ago. Kim Youmans is a former manager of the Hotel and worked there for nearly ten years. During that time, Kim reports that she and others experienced a number of unexplained happenings which they believe may have been caused by Matilda. Although she never saw an actual apparition, Kim says that Matilda had no trouble making her presence known.

Footsteps were regularly heard on the second floor of the Hotel when no living person was up there, and every so often Kim noticed "a cold breeze" blow past her, from no apparent source. One morning when she was working in the downstairs parlor, Kim clearly heard the sound of the rocking chair creaking in one of the second floor bedrooms. When she went up to investigate, the sound stopped. As Kim sat down on the rope bed for a moment to see if the sound would start up again, she noticed that the Victorian-style ladies fan that had been decorating the nightstand was missing. The fan was later discovered neatly folded in the nightstand drawer.

Kim recalls that a certain cupboard door would frequently open by itself. One day after she had closed the door several times, a co-worker advised her to "tell Matilda there is nothing in there she needs." Kim did so, and the door stayed closed the rest of the day.

Matilda, if that is indeed who she is, also seems to have a sense of humor. Kim remembers talking about the haunting with another employee in the Hotel kitchen. "I had just said something like, 'I really don't mind the things that go on here, unless pans start flying off the shelves or something.' At that exact moment, an entire stack of pans fell off the shelf."

Others entering the Hotel have also sensed the presence of a spirit or spirits. A female patron once told Kim, "there are other beings here" that raised the hair on the back of her neck. A co-worker's baby was observed waving at someone who could not be seen by the adults in the room.

Kim believes there is another, possibly male, spirit haunting the Hotel along with Matilda. Staff members have heard their names being called, and when female staff are alone in the building some have reported hearing a "wolf whistle" coming out of nowhere. An apparition of a soldier was once seen walking across the kitchen floor and then disappearing through a closed door.

Despite all of the ghostly activity she experienced while working at the Hotel, Kim maintains that she was never frightened. "I think Matilda must be Irish," Kim joked. "You should see what she does on Saint Patrick's Day!"

The Eagle Hotel

ACKNOWLEDGEMENTS

This book would not have been possible without the help of so many others, and I would like to take this opportunity to thank the following individuals and groups for their help in providing story leads and historical information: Andrea and Bob Greene, Lewis Dove, Elizabeth Way, Eric Perrye, the Erie County Historical Society and Museums, Judy Faustine, the Fort LeBoeuf Historical Society, the Corry Public Library, the Corry Journal, and the West County Historical Association.

A special thanks to Amanda Wincik for her computer expertise, and to Zachary Wincik for the cover design.

Finally, to all of the individuals whose tales are contained in these pages, a heartfelt thank you for trusting me with your very personal stories and allowing me to include them in this book.

SOURCES

INTRODUCTION
Mike Hudson, *Corry Journal*, February 8, 1992

THE BATTLES MUSEUMS
N.A. Reiter and L.L. Schillig, *The Enigmas of Girard, Pennsylvania*, November 24, 2002
Information provided by the Erie County Historical Society and Museums
Author's personal files

DEAD MAN'S CREEK
Local legend

POP
Personal interviews with Carl and Susan Sanders (pseud.,) February 2005, March 2005

LOIS
Telephone interview with Lois Bartos, January 2005

GRAVITY HILL
Local legend
International Directory of Magnetic Hills, Gravity Hills, Mystery Hills, and Magnetic Mountains, online source, August 2005

BETH'S HEARTS AND FLOWERS
Personal interview with Nancy Briody and Beth Gadley, May 2005

BOOM TOWN
Robin Dile Cuneo, "Corry History," *Erie Times News*, May 22, 1988
Telephone interview with Joni Chadwell, February 2005

SAUCERS
Personal interview with David Shaffer, January 2005

PREMONITIONS
Taped interview with Karen Luma, May 2005

OUIJA
Robert Todd Carroll, *The Skeptic's Dictionary*, online source, August 2005
Personal interview with Jason Gibbs, May 2005
Personal interview with Eric Perrye, August 2005

MORE SAUCERS
TourErie.com Communities, online source, July 2005
Telephone interview with Deb Perrye, January 2005

SPIRIT PHOTOGRAPHY
TourErie.com Communities, online source, July 2005
Personal interview with Bob and Cindy Riefstahl, April 2005

THE EAGLE HOTEL
Bootscooters.com, *A Short History of Waterford*, online source, August 2005
Information provided by the Fort LeBoeuf Historical Society
Personal interviews with Waterford residents
Telephone interview with Kim Youmans, August 2005

ABOUT THE AUTHOR

Stephanie Wincik is a lifelong resident of Girard, Pennsylvania. She holds a degree in Nursing from Penn State Behrend and is employed as a nursing supervisor at Erie Homes for Children and Adults, Inc.

Currently president of the West County Historical Association, Stephanie is also an active volunteer at the Battles Museums of Rural Life in Girard. She has published several articles about Girard in the Pennsylvania Magazine and writes a monthly column, "Local History Corner," for the West County News Journal.

Stephanie is the author of two other books, "Ghosts of Erie County," a collection of Erie County legends and supernatural tales, and "Northern Lights," a time travel adventure for young adult readers set during the Civil War.

www.ingramcontent.com/pod-product-compliance
Lightning Source LLC
Chambersburg PA
CBHW071635040426
42452CB00009B/1633